T0355653

ANTARCTICA

ANTARCTICA

LIFE ON THE FROZEN CONTINENT

CONOR KILGALLON

amber
BOOKS

Published by Amber Books Ltd
United House
North Road
London N7 9DP
United Kingdom
www.amberbooks.co.uk
Instagram: amberbooksltd
Facebook: amberbooks
Twitter: @amberbooks
Pinterest: amberbooksltd

Copyright © 2022 Amber Books Ltd.

All rights reserved. With the exception of quoting brief passages for the purpose of review
no part of this publication may be reproduced without prior written permission from the
publisher. The information in this book is true and complete to the best of our knowledge.
All recommendations are made without any guarantee on the part of the author or publisher,
who also disclaim any liability incurred in connection with the use of this data or specific details.

ISBN: 978-1-83886-197-1

Project Editor: Michael Spilling
Designer: Keren Harragan
Picture Research: Justin Willsdon

Printed in China

Contents

Introduction

Antarctica is a place of endless fascination – and extremes. Surrounded by the Southern Ocean and about twice the size of Australia, this huge continent is almost entirely covered in ice, at an average thickness of nearly 2km (1.2 miles). It claims the lowest temperature ever recorded on Earth, at -89.2°C (-128.6°F). On average, it's also the windiest and driest – it's actually a polar desert.

For centuries, Europeans wondered about the existence of a huge mythical continent in the south seas, calling it

Terra Australis. But it wasn't until the 19th century that sealers, whalers and explorers, whose exploits made them famous, mapped the real continent, and the race to claim territory and be the first to the South Pole was on.

This extreme environment has meant only a few animals have adapted to life here: seals, penguins, orcas and some seabirds have thrived, while migratory whales feed on krill. But, as climate change takes hold, a new race, to save this frozen wonderland, is on.

ABOVE:
Emperor penguin and chicks
The biggest – and hardiest – of all the penguin species, emperor penguins go to extreme lengths to breed. Chicks stay with their parents for around 50 days before forming a crèche with other offspring.

OPPOSITE:
Antarctica from Space
This fabled frozen continent, the fifth biggest on the planet, holds 70 per cent of the world's freshwater as ice. If all of it melted, global sea levels would rise by about 60m (200ft).

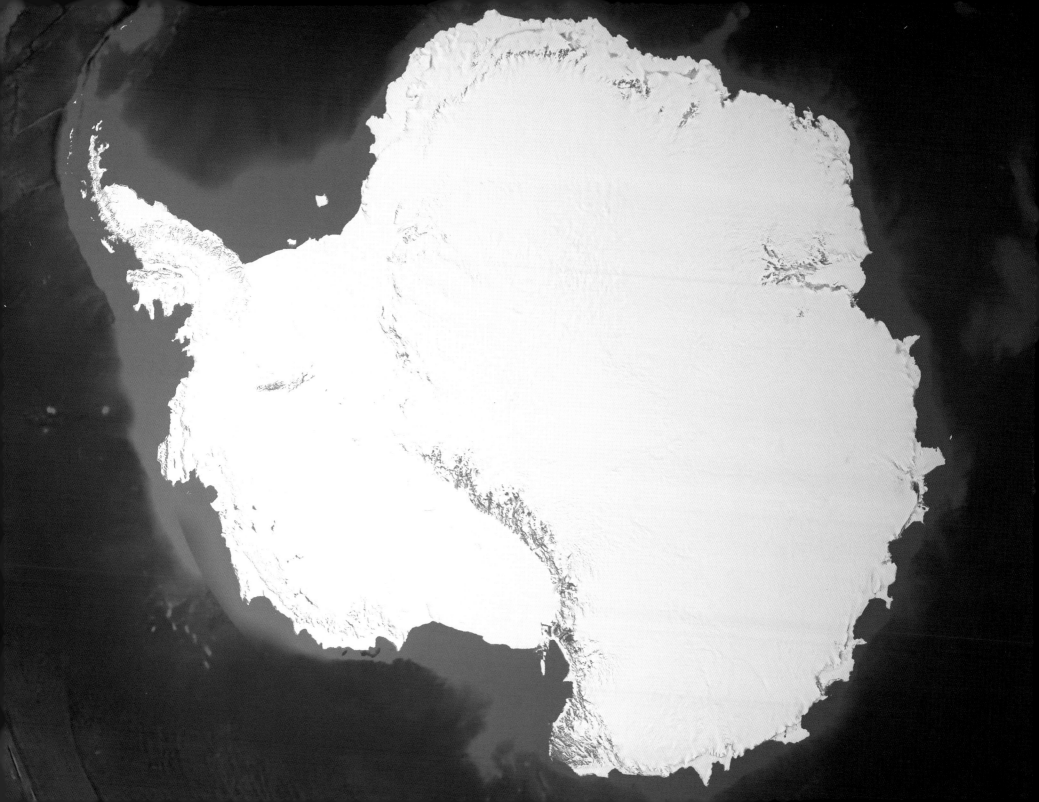

East Antarctica

Also known as Greater Antarctica, East Antarctica makes up about two-thirds of this vast continent and is almost entirely in the Eastern Hemisphere. The interior is predominantly covered in an ice sheet, making it a dramatic frozen wilderness with little in the way of plant or animal life. It also hosts the fabled South Pole, the subject of so many explorers' tales. But coastal areas see more activity and are the breeding ground for seabirds and the millions of penguins who live on or around the pack ice. Many seal species live in the freezing waters – Weddell seals, elephant seals and leopard seals can all be found hauled-out on rocks and the ice, and whales and orcas are visitors, too.

The coast of East Antarctica has also been widely visited and mapped, mainly during the 19th and 20th centuries, with explorers, sealers, whalers and scientists mostly arriving from Europe – Britain, France, Germany, Belgium, Russia and the Scandinavian countries all sent major expeditions thousands of miles south, along with significant US expeditions in the mid-20th century. They often stayed for several perilous years, and named sections of coastline in honour of their patrons, kings and queens, and after famous expedition leaders.

The huge glaciers and ice shelves on the East coast initially made finding somewhere to dock a ship problematic. Now, research stations dot the coast, belonging to various nations, wherever they can find a gap.

Different countries have territorial claims on the East Antarctic coastline, governed by the Antarctic Treaty. Australia claims the lion's share, with Norway next and France staking a small slice, too.

OPPOSITE:
Taylor Valley and Mummy Pond
Set in the Transantarctic Moutains in Victoria Land, the Taylor Valley is one of three extremely 'dry' (almost ice-free) valleys in the region. Named after an Australian geologist, Thomas Griffith Taylor, the valley does feature some water, such as Mummy Lake, which was named after the mummified seals found around the water's edge.

OPPOSITE:
Asgard Range, Victoria Land
Named in the 1950s after the home of the Norse gods, this
range of mountains contains lots of peaks, valleys and
glaciers, many of which are named after individual gods. Its
highest peak is Mount Thor, which rises to 1,812m (5,945ft).

ABOVE:
Mount Herschel, Victoria Land
Standing above Cape Roget in the Admiralty Range, Mount
Herschel was named in 1841 after Sir John Herschel, a famous
astronomer, who also promoted the exploration of the
Antarctic in the 19th century.

OPPOSITE AND ABOVE:
**Adélie penguin colony,
Adélie Land**
A huge colony of Adélie
penguins inhabit the rocks
below the French Dumont
d'Urville Antarctic base. The
Antarctic is the only place
Adélie penguins can be found,
and these colonies can grow
to 250,000 birds.

LEFT:
Adélie penguin study
A scientist examines a
penguin chick, which will
grow to become a 46–71cm
(18–28in) adult, as part of a
marine study. There are about
3.8 million of these penguins
in over 250 colonies.

**Tabular iceberg,
Dumont d'Urville Sea**
A huge tabular iceberg drifts
in the freezing sea. These
icebergs, also known as
table icebergs, are so-called
because of their flat tops and
vertical sides. They break off
(or 'calve') from the main ice
shelf and can be the size of
a small country – the 'B-15'
was 11,000 sq km (4,247 sq
miles). Some can be 300m
(1,000ft) high, though only
a tenth of its height may be
visible above water.

RIGHT AND OPPOSITE:

The Midnight Sun
Antarctica's summer runs
from October to February,
before winter kicks in again.
Being so far south, in mid-
summer the sun doesn't set
at all, creating the fabled
Midnight Sun. As the summer
gathers pace, these emperor
penguins get the chance to
enjoy some relatively balmy
temperatures of around
0°C (32°F).

Dibble Ice Shelf, Wilkes Land

This huge sheet of floating ice attached to the coastline was named after Jonas Dibble, a ship's carpenter on the *Peacock*. During the United States Exploring Expedition (1838–42), led by Captain Charles Wilkes, Dibble is credited with leaving his sick bed and working flat-out to repair the ship's broken rudder, which had been crushed by ice.

FAR RIGHT:

Vanderford Glacier

About 8km (5 miles) wide, this huge glacier was named after Benjamin Vanderford, pilot of the *Vincennes*, another ship in the United States Exploring Expedition (1838–42). The glacier is slowly sliding into a warming Southern Ocean, contributing to rising sea levels. The surface height of the glacier has dropped by more than 2m (6.6ft) since 2008, eaten away from below by warmer waters coming in from north of Antarctica.

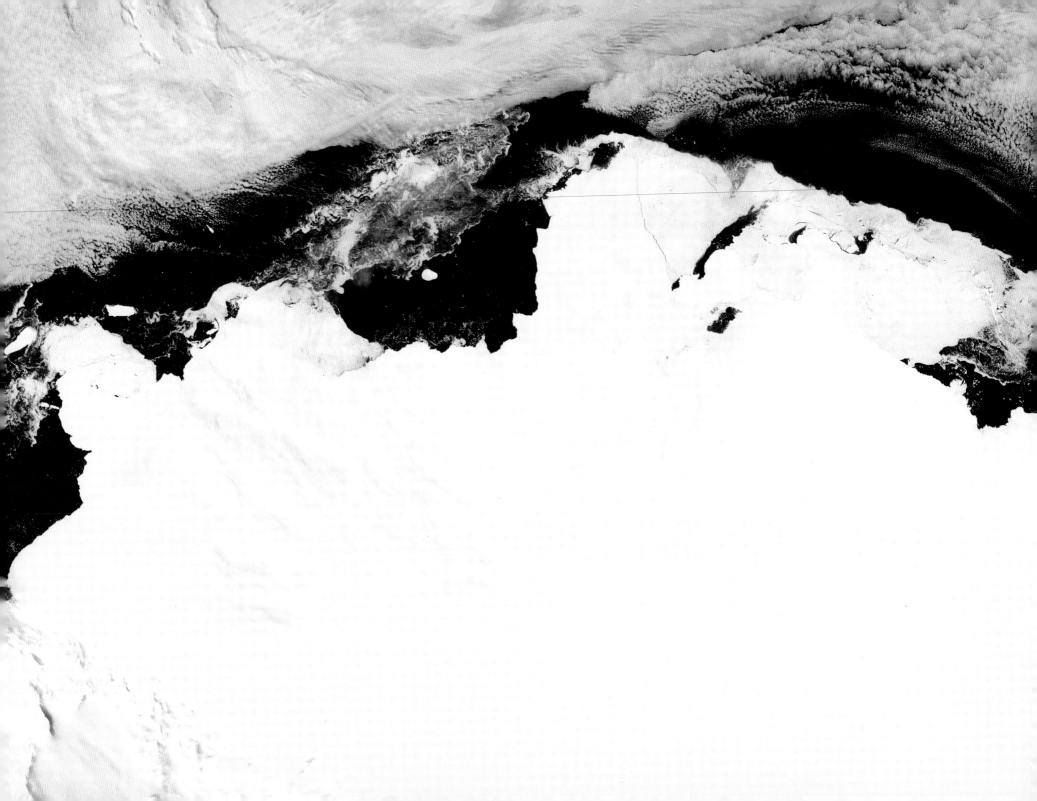

Queen Mary Land
Taken by NASA, this satellite image shows the coastline of
Queen Mary Land as it meets Davis Sea in the Southern Ocean.
This segment of East Antarctica is claimed by Australia as part
of the Australian Antarctic Territory, and was named for Mary,
wife of the British king, George V (1865–1936).

ABOVE:
Icebergs off Queen Mary Land
Pictured floating by in the Davis Sea near the Russian Mirny
polar station on the coast of Queen Mary Land, icebergs
in Antarctica form by breaking off, or 'calving', from the
continent itself. They pose a constant threat to shipping and
larger ones have to be tracked.

OPPOSITE:
Moonrise, Davis Sea
A red moon rises over an iceberg in the Davis Sea, another beautiful sight in this ice-covered wilderness.

LEFT:
Melting sea ice, Davis Sea
Freezing winter temperatures create so much sea ice that the continent of Antarctica almost doubles in size. But most of that sea ice melts and floats away during the summer months.

Emperor penguin colony, Davis Sea
A colony of emperor penguins sits on the sea ice with their
growing chicks. These iconic flightless birds are the biggest of
all the penguins and grow up to 100cm (39in) tall and can weigh
up to 45kg (99lb). To find the fish, krill and squid they live
on, emperor penguins can dive to extraordinary depths, 550m
(1,800ft) and hold their breath for 20 minutes, deeper and longer
than any other bird species.

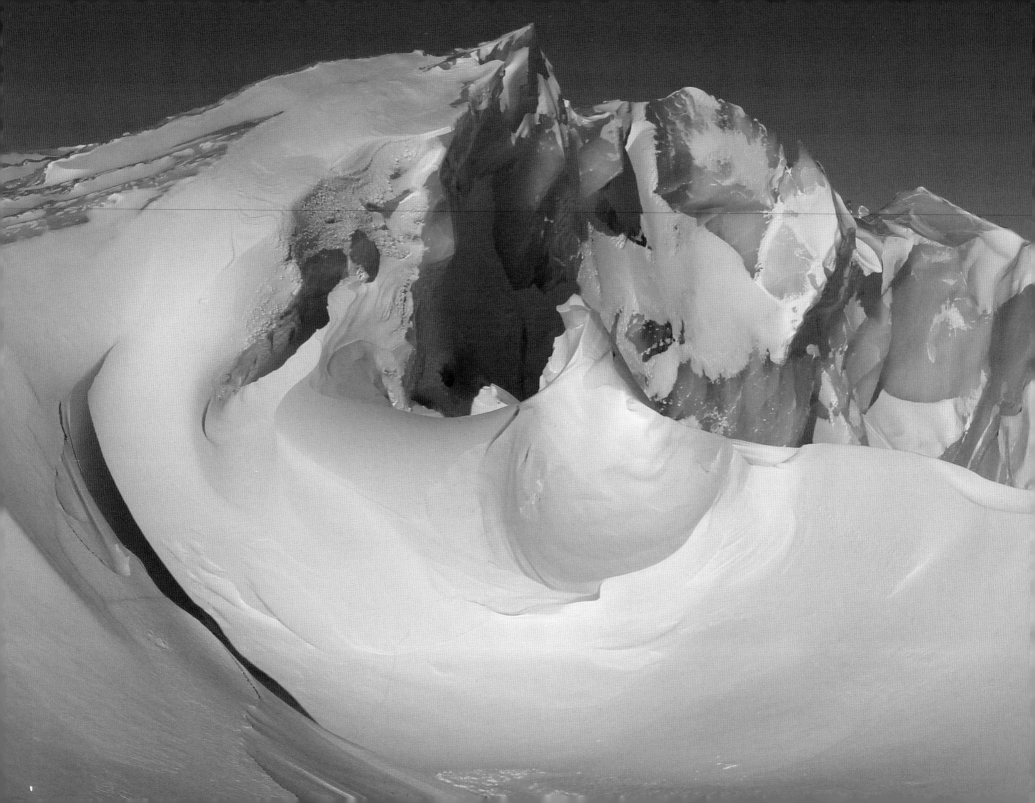

Iceberg, Davis Sea
In Antarctica, icebergs are made of freshwater ice that breaks off from an ice shelf or glacier and flows down to the sea. They become eroded by wind and water, which creates sculpted shapes. When winter arrives, they can get trapped in sea ice.

ABOVE:

Gaussberg, Kaiser Wilhelm II Land

The Gaussberg is a 370m (1,210ft) high extinct volcano, named after the mathematician and physicist, Carl Friedrich Gauss. The region was explored by geologist Erich von Drygalski in 1901–03, who named the entire area after Kaiser Wilhelm II, who had funded the expedition to the tune of over a million German marks.

RIGHT:

Davis Station, Princess Elizabeth Land

Forming one of three Australian Antarctic research bases, the Davis Station, or just 'Davis', sits on the coast of Cooperation Sea in an ice-free area called the Vestfold Hills. These ice-free areas are called 'Antarctic oases'. Davis studies viruses and bacteria, Antarctic marine ecosystems, atmospheric research and the structure of the East Antarctic ice sheet.

Progress Station, Prydz Bay
A propellor plane comes in
to land on a snow strip in
the Russian Progress Station.
This research base is set in the
Larsemann Hills Antarctic
oasis on the shore of Prydz
Bay. The station is capable of
staying open throughout
the winter.

Progress Station relics
The station was established
by the 33rd Soviet Antarctic
Expedition in 1988, and
later expanded to become a
support base. To be useful in
this climate, all vehicles had
to have caterpillar tracks and
heavy lifting abilities.

FAR LEFT:
Sunrise of over Progress Station, Prydz Bay
Not all research stations can stay open during the harsh winter but Progress Station can. It features a gym and sauna, together with a medical care unit that doubles up as a regional hospital. Up to 80 people are on-site at any one time.

LEFT:
Tide crack
This long straight crack is in 'fast ice', which is sea ice that has frozen to the land. But as the tide comes in and goes out again, the sea level rises and falls, cracking the ice. The tide crack pictured here is 8km (5 miles) long, but only about 50cm (20in) wide. Tide cracks help wildlife to feed – birds, such as snow petrels, can fish for krill, while crabeater and Weddell seals use the cracks as breathing holes.

ABOVE:

**Towing an 'apple hut', Mawson Station,
Australian Antarctic Territory**

In use since the mid-1980s, apple huts (or 'igloo satellite cabins') are lightweight shelters. Named after their shape and colour, these fibreglass rigid tents are easy to transport and build and can be erected by two people in under two hours. They can sleep three people, but in an emergency up to 15 can squeeze in.

RIGHT:

**A Weddell seal in front of RSV Australis,
Mawson Station**

Weddell seals are very common in the Antarctic and were named in the 1820s after British sealing captain, James Weddell. They can often be found around research stations. Here, one is 'hauled out' in front of the RSV Aurora Australis icebreaker as it visits Mawson Station, in the Australian Antarctic Territory. Mawson has been active since 1954.

Prince Charles Mountains, Mac. Robertson Land
This mountainous landscape features several ranges, including Athos, Porthos and Aramis. The highest peak in the region is Mount Menzies at 3,228m (10,590ft). The section shown here has a glacier between the mountains.

Icebergs off West Ice Shelf
An ice shelf is a large sheet of floating ice attached to a main mass of land. The West Ice Shelf is one of the biggest in East Antarctica, covering an area of 16,370 sq km (6,320 sq miles). Icebergs 'calve off' from these ice shelves.

LEFT:

Fog over Lambert Glacier, Amery Ice Shelf

The Lambert Glacier is the largest and fastest-moving glacier in the world, at about 80km (50 miles) wide, 400km (250 miles) long and 2.5km (1.6 miles) deep. It flows from the interior northward to the Amery Ice Shelf at a rate of up to 800m (2,620ft) per year.

RIGHT:

Jumping emperor penguin

To get themselves over the lip of thick ice sheets, emperor penguins, like many other penguins, can jump several feet out of the water. To help them make the leap, they cloak themselves in air bubbles collected by their feathers when they're swimming. This reduces friction between the penguin and the water, so when they swim fast to the surface, they are better able to burst out of the sea.

BOTH PHOTOGRAPHS:

Riiser-Larsen Ice Shelf, Weddell Sea

Set on the coast of Queen Maud Land, the Riiser-Larsen Ice
Shelf is about 400km (250 miles) long. Named after Captain
Hjalmar Riiser-Larsen, a Norwegian who explored the area
in the early 1930s, the ice shelf is an important area for
birds because it supports a breeding colony of about 4,000
emperor penguins.

Iceberg, Lazarev Sea
An iceberg with a top featuring lots of domes floats in the Lazarev Sea, off Princess Astrid Coast. While tabular icebergs have flat tops and sides, non-tabular ones are eroded into amazing shapes by water and wind.

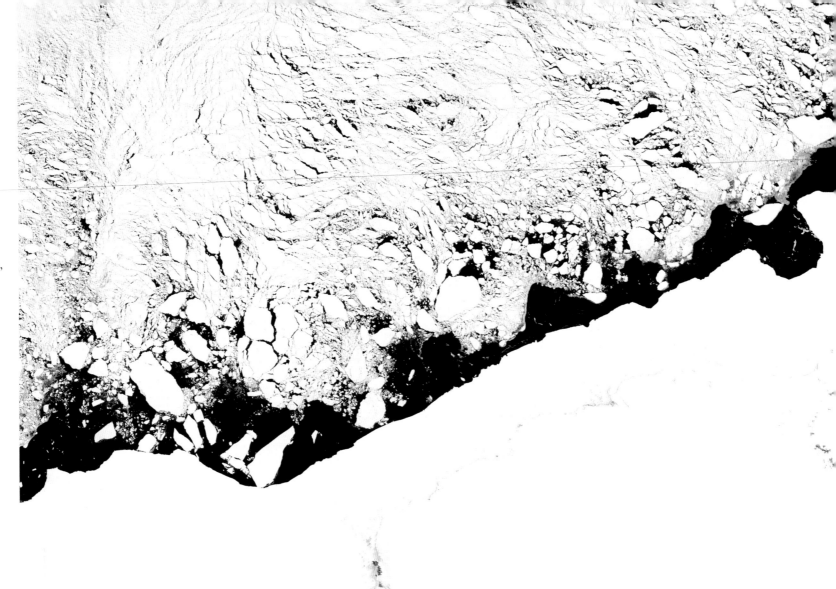

ALL PHOTOGRAPHS:
Prince Olav Coast
Explored by the Norwegian
Captain Hjalmar Riiser-
Larsen in January 1930,
this coast (right), a portion
of Queen Maud Land, was
named for the future King
Olav V of Norway.

As the summer gathers
pace, sea ice (called 'fast
ice' where it attaches to
land) breaks up and icebergs
(opposite left) start to move.
But when the fast ice is frozen,
icebergs remain trapped
(opposite right).

Fimbul Ice Shelf, Princess Martha Coast
At 200km (120 miles) long and 100km (60 miles) wide, the massive Fimbul Ice Shelf is fed by the Jutulstraumen Glacier, on the coast of Queen Maud Land. It was photographed and mapped by German, Norwegian, British and Swedish explorers and cartographers from the late 1930s to the late 1950s. Its name is taken from 'Fimbulisen', which means 'giant ice'.

Queen Maud Land coast

Claimed by Norway, after Captain Hjalmar Riiser-Larsen first arrived here in 1930, this vast region is about 2.7 million sq km (1 million square miles), making up about 20 per cent of the Antarctic continent. It's named after the Norwegian Queen Maud of Wales (1869–1938).

Most of the area is covered by the East Antarctic Ice Sheet, but there are peaks, too. The highest point is at Jøkulkyrkja (at 3,148m or 10,328ft) in the Mühlig-Hofmann Mountains. The coast consists of a 30m (100ft) wall of ice – ships can only dock in a few places.

LEFT:

Huddling emperor penguins

Male emperor penguins form a huddle to protect themselves, and the eggs they are incubating, against the fierce winter weather, where temperatures can dip to -40°C (-40°F). This huddling, known as social thermoregulation, allows the penguins to conserve body heat, with each penguin alternating between the outer edge and the warmer centre. Emperor penguins are the only penguins to breed in the winter.

ABOVE:

The South Pole, Antarctic Plateau

The geographic centre of the Southern Hemisphere, the fabled South Pole is on the Antarctic Plateau, the coldest part of the continent, at an altitude of 2,835m (9,301ft). The US Amundsen-Scott South Pole Station is set directly next to it. The exact spot is marked by the metal stake next to the US flag, and quotes from the two explorers who raced to the pole in 1911, Roald Amundsen and Robert F Scott, feature on the sign.

Halley VI Research Station, Caird Coast
The Aurora Australis puts on a winter show over the Halley Research Station on the Brunt Ice Shelf. Established in 1956 to study the Earth's atmosphere, measurements from Halley led to the discovery of the ozone hole in 1985. The base sits on a floating ice shelf in the Weddell Sea, so must be relocatable as the ice conditions change – its modular structure sits on huge hydraulic skis.

55

ALL PHOTOGRAPHS:

Coats Land, Antarctic Plateau

Named after James Coats Jr and Major Andrew Coats, two chief supporters of the Scottish National Antarctic Expedition that researched the area in 1902–04, Coats Land is part of the vast Antarctic Plateau (left), which is about 1,000km (620 miles) wide. This region includes the South Pole. Set at an average height of 3,000m (9,800ft), the plateau is one of the coldest places on Earth, once recording a temperature of -92°C (-134°F), meaning that only microbial life is possible. Ernest Shackleton was the first to cross parts of the Plateau in 1909 but had to turn back.

The coast of Coats Land includes the Brunt Ice shelf (above). Large cracks in the ice started to expand in around 2012, which meant that icebergs were likely to 'calve'. In 2021, a 1,270 sq km (490 sq mile) iceberg, named A-74, broke away.

ALL PHOTOGRAPHS:
Shackleton Range
Named after British explorer Ernest Shackleton, this mountain range peaks at Holmes Summit, at 1,875m (6,152ft). The range runs about 160km (99 miles) from east to west between the Slessor and Recovery Glaciers.

**The Amundsen–Scott
South Pole Station
Buckminster Fuller dome**
Set on the South Pole at a
height of 2,835m (9,301ft), the
American Amundsen–Scott
South Pole Station was the
first permanent structure at
the pole. In 1975, the iconic
Buckminster Fuller geodesic
dome was built, 50m (160ft)
wide and 16m (52ft) high, and
able to withstand the harsh
Antarctic Plateau winters,
where temperatures at the
dome could fall to -73°C
(-99°F). By 1998, the dome
started to crack and was
finally dismantled in 2009.

IceCube Neutrino Observatory, Amundsen–Scott South Pole Station
Completed in 2010 and run by the University of Wisconsin–Madison, the observatory is designed to measure neutrino subatomic particles coming from the sun, and thousands of sensors are located under the ice to detect them, covering one cubic kilometre (0.2 cubic miles). The IceCube is the largest neutrino telescope in the world.

Sea ice, Weddell Sea
Sea ice comes and goes during the year in Antarctica. Most of it – about 85 per cent – melts in the summer months, then refreezes during the winter. Because it never gets the chance to thicken year on year, Antarctic sea ice is rarely more than 1m (3ft) thick. The Weddell Sea maintains some sea ice, even in the summer.

OPPOSITE:

Iceberg, Weddell Sea
The summer months see the Antarctic sea ice break up and melt, freeing icebergs. Although the Weddell Sea maintains some of its ice, here, some Adélie penguins hitch a ride on a dome iceberg, looking like decorations on an iced cake.

RIGHT:

Sea ice, Weddell Sea
As winter takes hold, the sea ice freezes over all the way around the Antarctic, allowing these emperor penguins to form a colony. Icebergs also become trapped in the ice.

OVERLEAF:

Antarctic Peninsula mountains
Sea ice breaks up during the summer. Here the Weddell Sea has the dramatic, mountainous coastline of the Antarctic Peninsula in the background.

ABOVE:
Broken sea ice, Weddell Sea
East of the Antarctic Peninsula is the Weddell Sea, which retains much of its ice during the summer months. This is because cold winds blow up from the south, and a circular current, called a 'gyre', keeps the ice from drifting into the South Atlantic to the north.

RIGHT:
Rocky landmass
As some of the ice melts, it reveals rock beneath. This is a reminder that the Antarctic is a solid mass of land covered in ice, in direct contrast to the Arctic, which is an ocean with a large amount of frozen sea ice in the middle of it, surrounded by land.

Striped iceberg, Scotia Sea
The Scotia Sea is located between the Southern Ocean and the South Atlantic, and is an 'Iceberg Alley'. Almost all icebergs will pass through here, swept into this sea by a combination of the anti-clockwise Antarctic Coastal Current and the clockwise Antarctic Circumpolar Current. The black stripes on this iceberg are formed in glaciers as the moving ice picks up dirt and sediment on its way to the sea, before 'calving off' as an iceberg.

Cape petrel, Scotia Sea
With an estimated population of around two million, the Cape petrel is a very common seabird. During the breeding season, they arrive in Antarctica and the subantarctic islands, before heading north for winter, ending up in places such as Angola and the Galapagos Islands.

RIGHT:

Iceberg, Scotia Sea
Waves crash against a wedge
iceberg as it drifts in the
Scotia Sea. Most Antarctic
icebergs will transit through
this sea, after getting caught
in the currents that flow
around Antarctica – the anti-
clockwise Antarctic Coastal
Current and the clockwise
Antarctic Circumpolar
Current. The cave is caused
by sea water eroding the ice,
and the roof of the cave may
eventually collapse.

OPPOSITE:

Blue iceberg, Scotia Sea
An iceberg hints at the mass
of unseen ice below the
surface. Its blue colour is
caused by the absorption of
warm red wavelengths of
light, leaving icy blue as the
dominant colour.

ALL PHOTOGRAPHS:
Sculpted icebergs, Scotia Sea
The Scotia Sea sees a huge number of icebergs pass through it, as clockwise and anti-clockwise Antarctic ocean currents capture drifting bergs and push them northwards into the sea. As waves crash into the icebergs, they carve out shapes. Caves (opposite) are the most obvious, but other shapes form, too, such as the arch of this pinnacle iceberg (above). Mysterious-looking grottos (left) are eroded by wind.

West Antarctica

Also known as Lesser Antarctica, the western section of the continent makes up about one-third of its land mass, and lies in the Western Hemisphere. It's separated from East Antarctica by the Transantarctic Mountains, which run from Coats Land and the Weddell Sea, to the Ross Sea and Victoria Land.

Like East Antarctica, the West is covered by an ice sheet, but its climate is not so one-dimensional. The Antarctic Peninsula (with Graham Land forming the northern section and Palmer Land the southern part), juts into the Southern Ocean and comprises a series of mountainous islands, straits and bays, and, on its western and northern sides at least, has a relatively mild maritime climate. This milder environment creates more opportunity for life to thrive, and moss, lichens and algae can gain a toehold here during the short growing season. The less punishing climate also sees seabirds and penguins finding more spots to breed, while the waters host seals, orcas, whales, fish and krill.

The Antarctic Peninsula is also a natural stop-off point for cruises. Its proximity to South America, plus its plethora of beautiful sheltered bays and coves, makes it a real draw, as does the sealing, whaling and expeditionary history so evident in this part of Antarctica.

West Antarctica is one of the most rapidly warming areas in the world. This has a huge knock-on effect to the wildlife, and even species that thrive today face an uncertain future as the ice recedes. And as the giant ice shelves, such as those in the Weddell Sea and Ross Sea melt, releasing huge amounts of meltwater into the oceans, global sea levels rise.

As in the East, several nations claim territory here. Argentina, Great Britain, Chile and New Zealand have all planted their flags here.

OPPOSITE:
Icebergs, Antarctic Peninsula
The Antarctic Peninsula forms the northern-most part of the Antarctic mainland. It has a relatively mild climate compared to the rest of the continent and has been most affected by a warming climate, which in turn is having an impact on sea, bird and plant life.

BOTH PHOTOGRAPHS:

Icebergs, Antarctic Peninsula

Icebergs drift around the Antarctic Peninsula, some picking up passengers along the way. Smaller icebergs, around 1–5m (3.3–16ft) high and 5–15m (16–49ft) long are called 'bergy bits', or 'growlers', while others are truly gigantic, sometimes the size of a small country.

Antarctic Peninsula
Jutting out from the mainland, the mountainous Antarctic Peninsula is about 1,300km (810 miles) long and covers 522,000 sq km (202,000 sq miles). It is made up of a string of rocky islands joined together by an ice sheet, and which covers 80 per cent of its land surface.

RIGHT:

Icebergs, Andvord Bay
Pinnacle-shaped icebergs
float in Andvord Bay, on the
west coast of the Antarctic
Peninsula.

OPPOSITE:

Cruise ship, Neko Harbour
A cruise ship maneouvres
between the icebergs in Neko
Harbour, an inlet on Andvord
Bay. The harbour is a popular
tourist destination. In the
background is a glacier.

Bad weather in Neko Harbour, Antarctic Peninsula
A snowstorm blows in on the mountains surrounding the harbour. Although this part of Antarctica has seen warmer temperatures in recent decades, it's still very cold, barely creeping above freezing point in the summer and dropping to -20°C (-4°F) in the winter.

ABOVE AND RIGHT:

Danco Coast, Antarctic Peninsula
Featuring many bays and inlets, the beautiful Danco Coast
was named after Lieutenant Emile Danco, a member of
the Belgian Antarctic Expedition, who died here in 1898.
The Antarctandes mountain range rises behind this coast
and forms the backbone of the Antarctic Peninsula. These
mountains are actually the continuation of the South
American Andes.

OPPOSITE:

**Drake's Passage,
South Shetland Islands**
This body of water connects
the South Shetland Islands
in the Southern Ocean that
surrounds Antartica with
the south Pacific and south
Atlantic, as they converge
around Cape Horn off the tip
of South America. It's one of
the most treacherous passages
of water in the world, and
was named after the 16th-
century English sailor, Sir
Francis Drake.

RIGHT:

**Mountain peak,
Antarctic Peninsula**
A *nanatuk*, or mountain
peak, projects through the
permanent ice sheet. The
word comes from the Inuit
language from the Arctic
in Greenland.

Neko Harbour,
Andvord Bay
In summer, the sea ice melts, which allows cruise ships to enter the harbour. Named after the Scottish *Neko* whaling ship, the inlet is populated with humpback whales, gentoo penguins and Weddell seals, making it one of the most scenic places to arrive by ship in the world.

LEFT:

Iceberg, Andvord Bay

On calm days, and when most of the sea ice has melted, the reflections in the water in Andvord Bay are stunning, mirroring snow-covered mountains, glaciers flowing down to the sea and icebergs.

ABOVE:

Drift ice, Hughes Bay, Danco Coast

Named after Edward Hughes, captain of a sealing ship that sailed in these waters in the mid-1820s, this bay is reputed to be the site of the first landing on the Antarctic mainland, on 7 February 1821, by crew from the US sealing ship *Cecilia*, captained by John Davis.

Gentoo penguins, Cuverville Island
Lying in the Errera Channel off the west coast of the Antarctic Peninsula, Cuverville Island (or Île de Cavelier de Cuverville) is a rocky spot. It is designated as an Important Bird Area because of its gentoo penguins – there are about 6,500 breeding pairs in this colony.

LEFT:

Esperanza Base, Hope Bay, Trinity Peninsula
This permanent Argentinian research base in Hope Bay on Graham Land in the Antarctic Peninsula is a year-round station with about 50 residents, including children and school teachers. The base welcomes over a thousand visitors each year.

RIGHT:

Helicopter, Esperanza Base, Hope Bay, Trinity Peninsula
An Argentinian Sea King helicopter manoeuvres a container on to the base. Helicopters like these are used for moving cargo, and are prepared for search and rescue operations.

Fish Islands, Prosect Point, Graham Land

This isolated group of islands was first charted in the 1930s and are known, along with the Minnows, which are smaller islands to the east, for their 4,000 breeding pairs of Adélie penguins.

OPPOSITE:

Fuel barrels, Antarctic Peninsula

Rusty old fuel barrels are a problem in the Antarctic as they leak toxic chemicals into the ice and the ocean. There are an estimated 300,000 tonnes (295,000 tons) of rubbish in Antarctica, some of it more than a century old, and most of it produced by the research stations on the continent. Some of it cannot be seen or recovered as it's buried under the ice.

LEFT:

San Martin Base, Graham Land

Built in 1951, this Argentinian research station was the first human settlement south of the Antarctic Circle. This coastal region of Antarctica has a more moderate climate than the interior, and as temperatures here now rise to several degrees above freezing in the summer, some rain can fall.

ABOVE:

The *Europa*, Orne Harbour, Graham Land

The three-masted Dutch tall ship, the *Europa*, sits at anchor in Orne Harbour in February 2011. As with Neko Harbour, Orne is a popular site for tourist expeditions. This particular ship, a 'bark' (meaning it has three masts), has a steel hull and sails around the world.

Icebergs, Petermann Island
Some icebergs can get trapped against the coastline and can stay there for many years, like these on Petermann Island, before breaking free and drifting out to sea again. As well as icebergs, this island, like many near it off Graham Land in the Antarctic Peninsula, is also an Important Bird Area because of its 3,000 breeding pairs of gentoo penguins. The island also hosts an Argentinian hut, or refuge, which was built in the middle of the penguin colony.

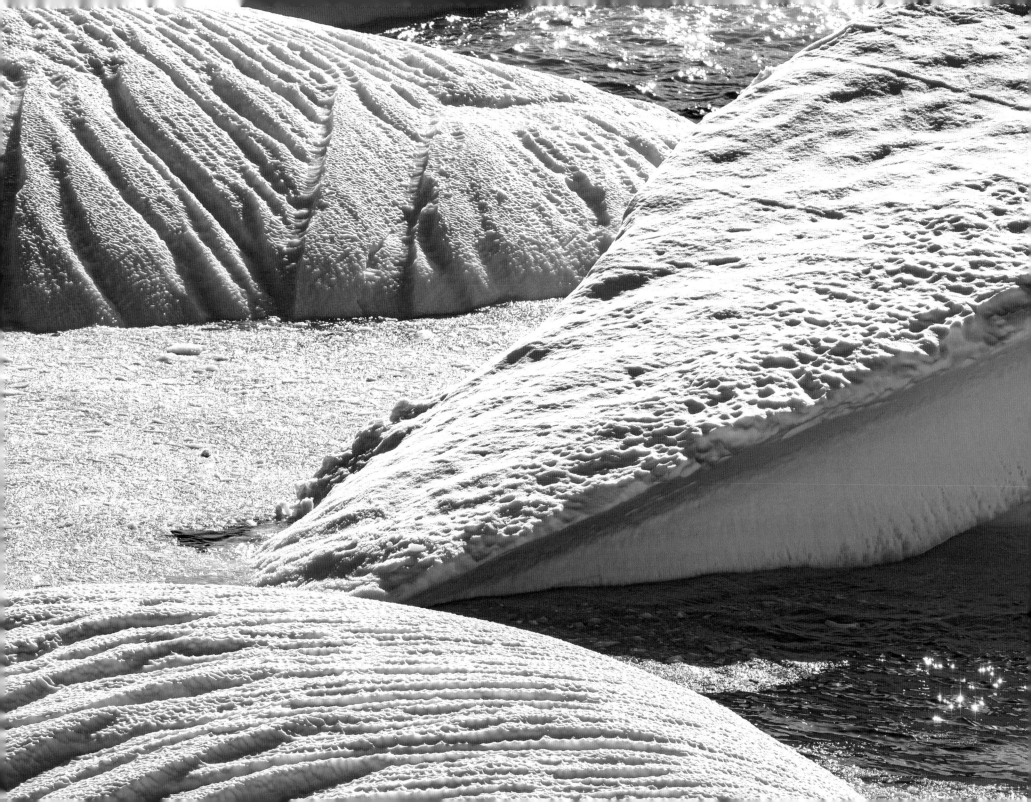

BOTH PHOTOGRAPHS:
**Lemaire Channel,
Graham Land**
One of the top spots in
Antarctica for visitors, the
narrow Lemaire Channel is
between the Kyiv Peninsula
and Booth Island. Dubbed
'Kodak Gap' for its beautiful
scenery, it's only 1.6km (1
mile) wide and features steep
mountains on either side,
and plenty icebergs.

ABOVE:

Bismarck Strait, Lemaire Channel, Graham Land
The Bismarck Strait marks the entrance to the Lemaire
Channel, and its mountains are awe inspiring. The channel was
named after Charles Lemaire (1863–1925), a Belgian explorer.

RIGHT:

Lemaire Channel, Graham Land
The channel is 11km (7 miles) long but its waters are well away
from the turbulence of the Southern Ocean. On a clear day,
when there's little wind or ice, the reflections are spectacular.

East Base, Stonington Island, Marguerite Bay
Commissioned by Franklin D. Roosevelt in 1939, the East Base
is the oldest US research base in Antarctica. Built using former
Army huts, the base was evacuated in 1941 due to World War
II and the difficulty of supplying the base, because of pack ice
in the bay. It was reopened in 1947 before being finally closed
in 1948. It's now visited by tourists to the region.

ABOVE:
**British Antarctic Survey Station E, Stonington Island,
Marguerite Bay**
The British Station E was built just 230m (250yd) from the US
East Base. It was manned from 1946–50, then again for a year
in the late 1950s, before staying open from 1960–75. During this
time it used some of the buildings from the US East Base as a
storehouse. As with East Base, Station E is now a tourist site.

Marguerite Bay, Antarctic Peninsula
On the west side of the Antarctic Peninsula, Marguerite
Bay is set between Adelaide Island, and Wordie Ice
Shelf, George VI Sound and Alexander Island. The bay
was discovered by the French Antarctic Expedition in
1909, whose leader, Jean-Baptiste Charcot, named it
after his wife.

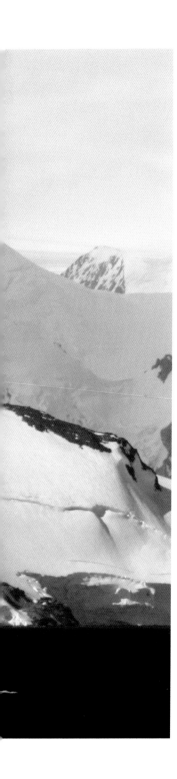

**Marguerite Bay,
Antarctic Peninsula**
A large weathered, pinnacle
iceberg floats in Marguerite
Bay, with the mountains of
the Antarctic Peninsula in the
background.

**Marie Byrd Land,
West Antarctica**
Although explored in
the early 20th century by
American naval officer
Richard E. Byrd, who named
the region after his wife,
this huge area is officially
unclaimed by any nation. It
sits east of the Ross Ice Shelf
and its vast 1.6 million sq km
(620,000 sq mile) expanse is
covered by the West Antarctic
Ice Sheet. It also hosts the
lowest point on the continent,
the Bentley Subglacial
Trench, at 2,555m ((8,327ft)
below sea level.

At 2,705m (8,875ft), Mount
Murphy (pictured opposite
top) is one of the highest
peaks in West Antarctica.

A-68 iceberg, Antarctic Peninsula

The western edge of the giant A-68 tabular iceberg, which 'calved' from the Larsen C Ice Shelf on the Antarctic Peninsula in July 2017. One of the biggest icebergs ever seen, this massive sheet of ice was 5,800 sq km (2,200 sq miles), approximately twice the size of Luxembourg. By April 2021, this giant iceberg had broken up, with the largest fragment only 5.5km (3.5 miles) long.

Sea ice, Antarctic Peninsula

Broken summer sea ice floats around a group of islands, as seen from NASA's Operation IceBridge research aircraft off the coast of the Antarctic Peninsula in 2017.

LEFT:
Cruise ship, Paradise Bay, Antarctic Peninsula
A cruise ship stops its engines so tourists can have a peaceful view of this deep water bay. The name was coined by whalers in the early 1920s.

ABOVE:
Brown Station, Paradise Bay, Antarctic Peninsula
Established in 1951, this summer-only Argentinian research station is one of 13 in the Antarctic and sits on a rocky outcrop in the bay. It's sheltered from strong winds by the nearby mountains. About 18 people live on the base, which is also visited by tourists arriving by boat.

ABOVE:
**Mountains, Paradise Bay,
Antarctic Peninsula**
This is a popular harbour and regularly sees humpback
whales and seals in its waters, plus gentoo penguins, petrels
and terns on the coast.

RIGHT:
**Refuge Conscripto Ortiz, Paradise Harbour,
Antarctic Peninsula**
Run by the Argentinian Navy since 1956, this refuge is named
after a conscript, Mario Inocencio Ortíz, who died in naval
service. Set 230m (251yd) from Brown Station, the refuge
was used as a meteorological observatory and as a base for
Antarctic exploration.

Iceberg, Paradise Harbour, Antarctic Peninsula
An iceberg sits in Paradise Harbour, its beautiful serrated shape created by wind erosion. Shapes like these, when found on glaciers, are called séracs.

Suárez Glacier, Skontorp Cove, Graham Land
Originally known as Petzval Glacier, this glacier was remapped and renamed by a Chilean Antarctic expedition in the early 1950s. The glacier runs down to Skontorp Cove in Paradise Harbour from an elevation of 861m (2,825ft).

ABOVE:

Iceberg, Pléneau Bay, Wilhelm Archipelago
Another tourist hotspot for cruise ships visiting the Antarctic Peninsula that want to see gentoo penguins and icebergs sculpted by the wind, Pléneau Bay was named after Paul Pléneau, photographer of the French Antarctic Expedition, 1903–05, which was led by famous French explorer, Jean Baptiste Charcot.

RIGHT:

Gentoo penguins, iceberg A57A, Larsen Ice Shelf, Antarctic Peninsula
Set in the northwest part of the Weddell Sea, the Larsen Ice Shelf is a series of shelves that once covered 85,000 sq km (33,000 sq miles). Due to global warming, giant icebergs have since 'calved off', including the A57A, reducing its overall size to 67,000 sq km (26,000 sq miles).

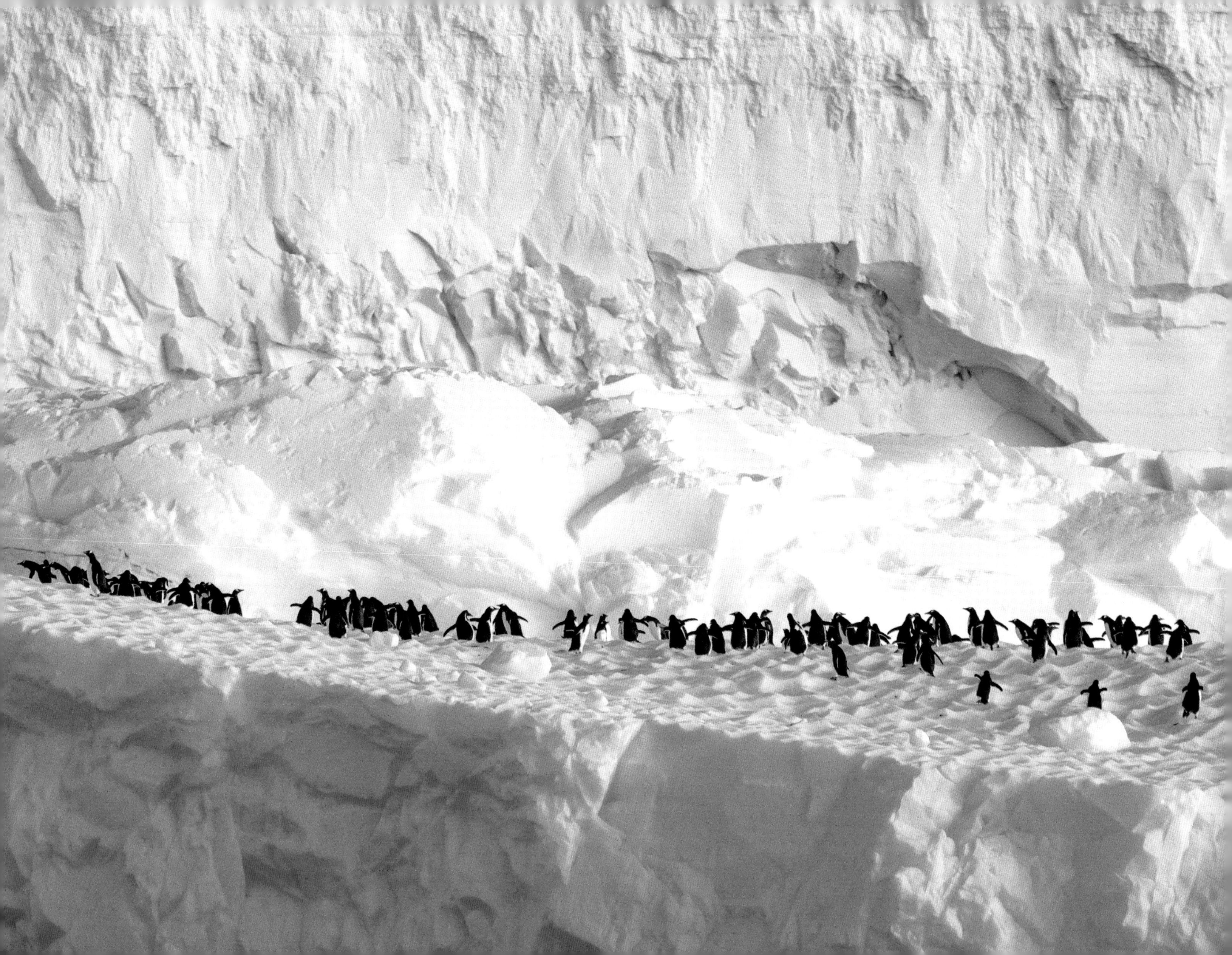

RIGHT:

Larsen Ice Shelf, Weddell Sea, Antarctic Peninsula
This vast ice shelf sits in the Weddell Sea, off the northeast coast of the Antarctic Peninsula. It's made up of four main sections, A, B, C and D, the first three of which have begun disintegrating over the last 30 years due to climate change.

OPPOSITE:

Larsen A Ice Shelf, Weddell Sea, Antarctic Peninsula
Of the four main parts of the ice shelf, Larsen A is the smallest. It disintegrated in January 1995, followed by large parts of Larsen B in early 2002. Larsen C, the biggest section, 'calved off' the giant A-68 iceberg in July 2017, which was 5,800 sq km (2,200 sq miles) and more than 200m (700ft) thick. Larsen D remains stable.

Larsen Ice Shelf, Weddell Sea, Antarctic Peninsula
The vast Larsen Ice Shelf is just one of several in the Antarctic, but is one that is disintegrating fast. The Antarctic Peninsula has warmed by nearly 3°C (5.3°F) over a 50-year period from the early 1950s, faster than the rest of the continent and higher than the global trend. If all the ice in the Larsen C shelf were to melt, global sea levels would rise by about 10cm (4in).

**Neumayer Channel,
Palmer Archipelago,
Antarctic Peninsula**
Named after Georg von
Neumayer by Belgian
explorer Adrien de Gerlache
on his 1897–99 expedition,
the 16-mile Neumayer
Channel, along with the
Lemaire Channel, is known
for its stunning views of
mountains, icebergs and ice
formations. Whales can be
spotted in its waters.

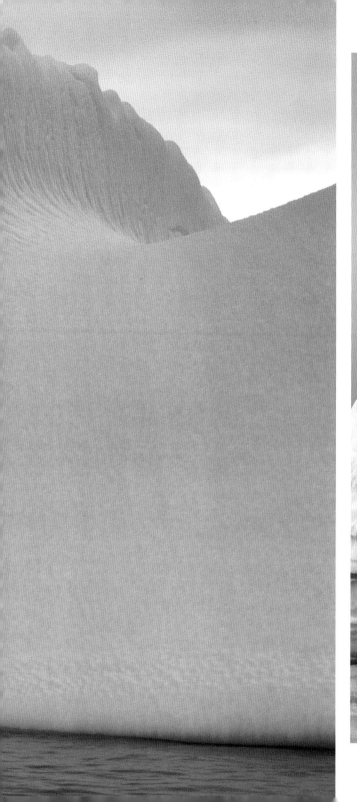

BOTH PHOTOGRAPHS
AND OVERLEAF:
**Icebergs in the
Gerlache Strait**
Beautiful and alluring iceberg
shapes in the Gerlache
Strait, a body of water that
separates the islands of the
Palmer Archipelago from the
Antarctic Peninsula.

ABOVE:

Hydruga Rocks, Palmer Archipelago, Antarctic Peninsula
Spectacular light during sunset over an iceberg and Hydruga Rocks in the Palmer Archipelago. The archipelago was named after American captain Nathaniel Palmer, who explored these waters in 1820.

OPPOSITE:

Whale skeleton, Port Lockroy, Palmer Archipelago
Forming a natural harbour, Port Lockroy is a bay on Wiencke Island. It was a safe anchorage for whaling fleets in the early 20th century, and later gave its name to the first continuously occupied British base in Antarctica in 1944. It's now a tourist spot with a living museum, post office and shop.

OPPOSITE:
Seven Sisters Mountains, Jougla Point, Port Lockroy, Palmer Archipelago
A string of rocky, snow-covered peaks above Port Lockroy on Wiencke Island, the Seven Sisters trail off along a serrated ridge from Savoia Peak, the island's high point at 1,415m (4,642ft).

RIGHT:
Iceberg, Bransfield Strait, Palmer Archipelago
A huge tabular iceberg drifts though the Bransfield Strait, which separates the South Shetland Islands from the Antarctic Peninsula.

BOTH PHOTOGRAPHS:

Base A, Port Lockroy
A colony of gentoo penguins surrounds Base A, Port Lockroy. This was a British base established in Feburary 1944 in the bay of the same name. The base is actually on a small island called Goudier Island in the bay, and includes the most southerly operational post office in the world. The base was established as a wartime mission named Operation Tabarin, which aimed to create a permanent British presence in Antarctica. The base later became a scientific research station and is now a historic site regularly visited by tours.

Ronne-Filchner Ice Shelf, Weddell Sea
At over 422,000 sq km (162,935 sq miles) and up to 600m
(1,968ft) thick, the Ronne-Filchner Ice Shelf is the second-
biggest in Antarctica, after the Ross Ice Shelf in the Ross Sea.
It sits in the Weddell Sea and is fed by ice running down the
Slessor Glacier, the Recovery Glacer and the Support Force
Glacier. Every few years giant icebergs break off, such as
the A-38, in October 1998, measured at 7,500 sq km (2,896
sq miles). The ice shelf is gradually melting and may have
disappeared by the end of the 21st century, which would add
40cm (15.5in) to global sea levels.

Bellingshausen Sea, Antarctic Peninsula
Set on the western edge of the Antarctic Peninsula, this sea has an area of 487,000 sq km (188,000 sq miles). The summer sees the sea ice melt, allowing cruise ships to cut through.

LEFT:

Bellingshausen Station, Maxwell Bay

Set on King George Island in the South Shetland Islands, this Russian research station was set up in 1968. It's open all year round, and has relatively mild weather, with average winter temperatures of -6.5°C (20.3°F)

ABOVE:

Trinity Church Bellingshausen Station, Maxwell Bay

Consecrated in 2004, this pine-built Eastern Orthodox church is one of eight churches in Antarctica. It can hold 30 worshippers of all denominations and is staffed year round.

ABOVE:

The Ellsworth Mountains, Ellsworth Land

Set on the western edge of the Ronne-Flischner Ice Shelf, the Ellsworth Mountains are made up of the Heritage Range to the south and the Sentinal Range to the north. These are the highest mountains in Antarctica and run for 350km (217 miles). Among the peaks is Mount Vinson, which at 4,892m (16,050ft) is the highest point in Antarctica.

RIGHT:

Russian transport aircraft, Union Glacier Blue-Ice Runway

A giant Ilyushin Il-76 transport sits on the ice runway at Union Glacier, near the Heritage Range section of the Ellsworth Mountains. Its job is to resupply the Union Glacier Camp, which is used seasonally to conduct tours to the Antarctic interior, including the South Pole. The glacier is also the site of the annual Antarctic Ice Marathon.

LEFT:

Union Glacier, Ellsworth Mountains

The glacier drains through the middle of the Heritage Range in the Ellsworth Mountains. Here, it appears to have waves on its snow-free surface, and has lots of crevasses. Elsewhere it is flat, and is the site of Union Glacier Blue-Ice Runway and Union Glacier Camp, which is a base camp for tours into the interior of the Antarctic.

ABOVE:

Behrendt Mountains, Ellsworth Land

The horseshoe-shaped Behrendt Mountains, a 32km (20 mile) long range in Ellsworth Land, contains Mount Abrams (pictured) and Mount Brice, and is situated at the base of the Antarctic Peninsula.

Getz Ice Shelf, Marie Byrd Land
Set on the West Antarctic coastline of Marie Byrd Land, the Getz Ice Shelf covers 32,810 sq km (12,668 sq miles). It has been gradually thinning out, producing more meltwater than any other ice sheet in the world.

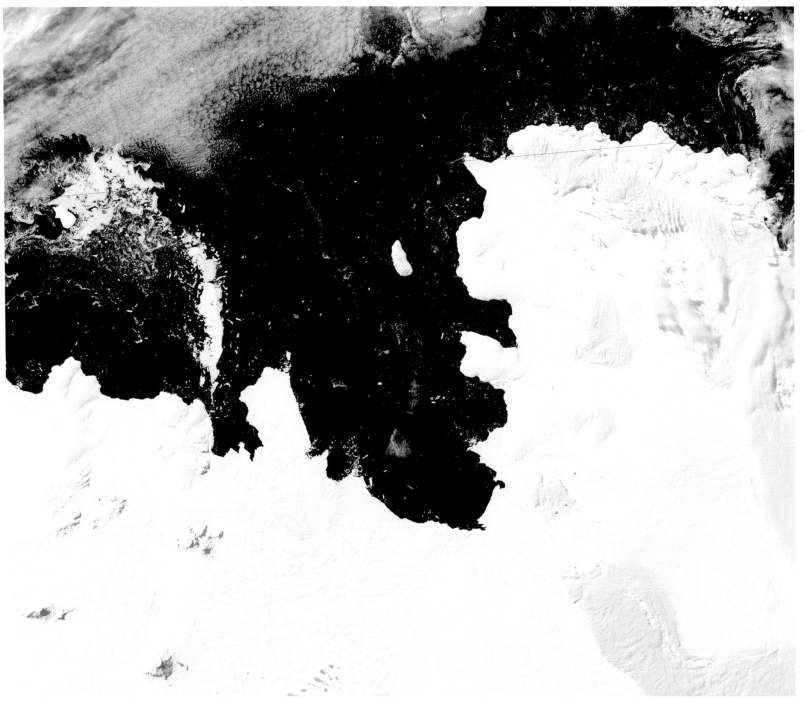

Pine Island Bay, Amundsen Sea

The bay receives ice streams from the Pine Island Glacier. This is the fastest-melting glacier in Antarctica, and accounts for roughly a quarter of Antarctica's ice loss. This loss has been happening since the 1940s, but has dramatically accelerated in the last 20 years.

OPPOSITE:

Mount Erebus, Ross Island, Ross Sea

Set on Ross Island, which is formed by four volcanoes, three of which are extinct, Mount Erebus is the most active volcano in Antarctica and regularly produces gas and steam. At 3,794m (12,448ft), members of Ernest Shackleton's Nimrod expedition climbed it in 1908. It has a lava lake in its crater. The mountain is named after HMS *Erebus*, one of Sir James Clark Ross's vessels during the Ross expedition, 1839–43.

Ross Ice Shelf, Ross Sea
The largest ice shelf in Antarctica, the Ross Ice Shelf is in the Ross Sea, the world's most southerly sea. At nearly 473,000 sq km (183,600 sq miles) it's roughly the size of Spain; it's also several hundred metres thick, with the vast majority of the ice underwater. The ice at the face is 15–50m (50–160ft) above the water line. This ice shelf contains enough water to raise sea levels by 15m (40ft) if it melted.

Icebreaker, Ross Sea
Sea ice is a serious problem for ships and can trap them for weeks. Powerful icebreakers have strengthened hulls and an icebreaking shape but can still get into trouble. The MV *Akademik Shokalskiy*, shown here in the Ross Sea, was trapped for two weeks in the ice in 2013, and all crew and passengers had to be evacuated.

Ross Ice Shelf, Ross Sea
Named after Sir James Clark Ross, the British naval officer and explorer who discovered it in January 1841, its vast height and size led Ross to call it the Barrier, or Great Ice Barrier, before it was renamed in Ross's honour.

ABOVE:

Ice in the Ross Sea

The Ross Sea is a vast 637,000 sq km (246,000 sq mile) body of water and has been called 'The Last Ocean', as it is the world's most southerly sea. It is covered with ice for most of the year but is full of life. Penguins, whales, seals, krill, sea birds and plankton all live around or in its waters.

OPPOSITE:

Transantarctic Mountains

At 3,500km (2,200 miles), the Transantarctic Mountains are one of the longest ranges in the world. They run from Coats Land to Cape Adare in Victoria Land. The highest peak is Mount Kirkpatrick, at 4,528m (14,856ft). Bitterly cold in the interior, only bacteria, lichens and algae can survive.

Islands

Antarctica's islands are often as famous as the main continental land mass itself, and several have a story to tell. Many islands are arrayed to the north and west of the Antarctic Peninsula, some as individual spots and others in groups a little further out, such as the South Orkneys and South Shetlands. Many are spectacular. The ones closest to the mainland are connected to it by pack ice, or are separated by a variety of channels, such as the Antarctic Sound, the Gerlache Strait and the cruise-boat friendly Lemaire Channel, depending on the time of year.

Many islands around the Antarctic Peninsula, by virtue of their location, were the first to be found by a variety of expeditions, some commercial, such as sealing and whaling, and some more scientific and exploratory. The 'Heroic Age of Antarctic Exploration' got going at the end of the 19th century and ended in 1917. During that time 17 major expeditions were launched from 10 countries. Many islands are named after these explorers and sealers, and the kings, queens and institutes that sent them south.

Not all islands are just mountainous rocks covered in ice. Deception Island is still volcanic and other subantarctic islands, such as the Falklands and South Georgia, are important nesting and breeding grounds for penguins and seabirds, as the climate is slightly less harsh.

And not all the islands are located around the Antarctic Peninsula, or out in the Southern Ocean. Ross Island sits in the Ross Sea, and is forever associated with Robert Falcon Scott and his ill-fated mission to the South Pole in 1911.

OPPOSITE:
Old whaling station, Deception Island
Set in the South Shetland Islands, Deception Island is close to the Antarctic Peninsula and has a natural central harbour. This volcanic island found its way on to the map during a short-lived sealing boom in the early 19th century, before becoming a whaling station about a century later. It is now a popular tourist destination, with over 15,000 visitors per year.

OPPOSITE:

Ice front, Adelaide Island
Mainly covered in ice,
Adelaide Island covers 5,143
sq km (3,195 sq miles), with
Mount Bodys rising to over
1,220m (4,000ft). The island
was named in honour of
Queen Adelaide, wife of
British king, William IV, by
the British explorer John
Briscoe, who discovered the
island in 1832.

LEFT:

**Antarctic fur seals,
Adelaide Island**
Thought to be the most
abundant species of fur seal,
with up to six million animals,
most Antarctic fur seals
actually spend their time in
the subantarctic islands, such
as South Georgia.

**George VI Ice Shelf,
Alexander Island**
The biggest island in
Antarctica, Alexander Island
covers 93,600 sq km (58,162
sq miles). It's separated from
Palmer Land on the Antarctic
Peninsula by George VI
Sound, which is entirely filled
by the George VI Ice Shelf.

OPPOSITE:

Alexander Island pollution
Dumped aviation fuel drums
litter the landscape on Fossil
Bluff on Alexander Island.
The same problem occurs in
other parts of Antartica.

166

LEFT:

Booth Island, Graham Land
Also called Wandel Island, this mountainous Y-shaped island is 8km (5 miles) long and sits off the northwest coast of Graham Land. Wandel Peak is the highest point on the island, at 980m (3,215ft).

ABOVE:

Sunset at Port Charcot, Booth Island, Graham Land
Set in Booth Island, Port Charcot is a bay 2.4km (1.5 miles) wide. It was named after French explorer and doctor, Jean-Baptiste Charcot, who established the third French Antarctic Expedition's winter base here in 1904.

De Gerlache Strait, Antarctic Peninsula
Separating the islands of the Palmer Archipelago from the Antarctic Peninsula, the De Gerlache Strait was explored by the Belgian Antarctic Expedition under Adrien de Gerlache in 1898, after whom the channel was eventually named.

LEFT:
Deception Island volcano
The island is so-named because it looks like a normal island, when in fact its centre is a 10km (6 mile) wide flooded caldera of an active volcano. The 'harbour' is accessed through a narrow opening at Neptune's Bellows – one of the only places on Earth where boats can sail into the centre of a volcano. The last eruption was as recent as 1969, and ash from this volcano has been found in ice at the South Pole.

Whaling, Deception Island
In the early 20th century, whalers moved in with hundreds of men on the island in the summer. A postal service and radio station were all present, before whale-processing was moved to ships and the island was deserted.

Sunset from Vernadsky Station, Galindez Island
Despite its location just off the coast of the Antarctic Peninsula, the climate here is classified as 'marine subantarctic', moderated by the Pacific Ocean. Winter temperatures bottom out at -20°C (-4°F).

Humpback whale, Greenwich Island
Set in the South Shetland Islands, Greenwich Island is 24km (15 miles) long. During the summer, this West Antarctic Peninsula region is visited by thousands of humpback whales, who come to feed on Antarctic krill.

LEFT:
Yankee Harbour, Greenwich Island
Known to both American and British sealers since the 19th century, Yankee Harbour is now an important site for breeding pairs of gentoo penguins. Southern elephant seals, Weddell seals and Antarctic fur seals are all also regular visitors.

Chinstrap penguins on Half Moon Island

Half Moon Island is a series of spits of land called tombolos that connect volcanic bedrock islands. The island is a stop-off for summer Antarctic cruises, allowing visitors to see the chinstrap penguins and a breeding colony of about 100 pairs of south polar skuas.

OPPOSITE:

James Ross Island

Named after Sir James Clark Ross, the leader of a British expedition to this area in 1842, this large island rises to 1,630m (5,350ft). Dinosaur fossils have been found here – two of only three known discoveries in Antarctica.

LEFT:

Mendel Polar Station, James Ross Island

The island hosts a Czech research station and, until 1995, was connected to the east coast of the Antarctic Peninsula by an ice shelf. The ice shelf then collapsed, making the Prince Gustav Channel that separates the island from the mainland passable for the first time.

Livingston Island

In 1819, Livingston Island became the first land discovered south of 60° south latitude, bringing an end to the search for the mythical *Terra Australis Incognita* (Unknown Southern Continent) and the beginning of our understanding of the real Antarctica.

Penguins, Livingston Island

There is lots of life on this island including chinstrap, gentoo, Adélie and macaroni penguins, as well as several species of seals – Weddell, fur, elephant and leopard. Seabirds such as skuas, southern giant petrel and Antarctic terns nest here in the summer.

ABOVE:
Stone hut, Paulet Island, Antarctic Peninsula
In 1903, the ship *Antarctic*, part of the Swedish Antarctic Expedition, was crushed by the ice and sank off the coast of this volcanic island. The survivors built a stone hut for shelter, and also created a large pile of stones (a cairn) on the highest point of the island to be visible to rescuers. These are all now historic sites.

RIGHT:
McMurdo Station, Ross Island, Ross Sea
Set on the tip of Ross Island, McMurdo Station is an American Antarctic research station, on the shore of McMurdo Sound. This year-round station has the biggest population in Antarctica, with over 1,200 residents.

OPPOSITE:

Main road, McMurdo Station, Ross Island
This United States' station is one of three year-round American research facilities, and is the biggest station of any kind in Antarctica, effectively the size of a small town. It's the gateway to the South Pole. To power the station, the US Navy installed a small nuclear power plant, but this was decommissioned just 10 years later, in 1972.

LEFT:

Pancake ice formation
This distinctive type of ice is formed when waves act on slushy ice or ice rind (a shiny crust of floating ice), creating these round shapes, like lily pads. Diameters can range from 30cm (12in) to 3m (10ft), with thicknesses of up to 10cm (4in), depending on sea conditions.

ALL PHOTOGRAPHS:
Scott's Hut, Ross Island
Built in 1911 at Cape Evans by the 'Terra Nova' British Antarctic Expedition led by Robert Falcon Scott ('Scott of the Antarctic'), the hut (opposite) was 15m (50ft) long and 7.6m (25ft) wide. With double insulated walls, heating came from the kitchen and a coal-fired stove (top left), while lighting was provided by acetylene gas. The hut also had separate areas for sleeping and working and had a utility room (bottom left).

Twenty-five men lived in the hut and it was from here that Scott and his men set out on their ill-fated trek to the South Pole, which they reached in January 1912. The hut was reused from 1915 to 1917 by several of Ernest Shackleton's Ross Sea party, before being abandoned. In 1956, US explorers dug it out of the snow and ice to find it well preserved.

OPPOSITE:

**Shackleton's Hut,
Cape Royds, Ross Island**

The base associated with
Brtish explorer Ernest
Shackleton was used during
the 'Nimrod' British Antarctic
Expedition in 1907–09, as he
attempted (but failed) to be
the first to reach the South
Pole. The hut was the home
of 14 men for 14 months. It
survives today, well-preserved.

RIGHT:

**Nordenskjöld Hut,
Snow Hill Island,
Antarctic Peninsular**

The island was used as a base
by the Swedish Antarctic
Expedition, which sailed in
the ship *Antarctic*, under
Otto Nordenskjöld. His party
spent the winters of 1901–03
there, exploring the region,
before building the wooden
hut (right) in 1902. The
Antarctic was crushed by ice
and sank in 1903.

Wildlife

It seems that wherever life can take hold, it will. And although there is very little biodiversity in Antarctica – only a few animals have adapted to survive the cold – life still thrives. But very little can exist in the interior of the continent, which is covered with an ice sheet, and has some of the coldest temperatures on the planet. On these frozen wastes, temperatures can drop to around -90°C (-130°F). Here, only bacteria can exist, not just because of the low temperatures but because of the incredible dryness – Antarctica is a desert.

But move to the coasts and the story changes dramatically. Here, with less extreme temperatures and access to the ocean, dozens of seabirds and five species of penguin (for a total of about 20 million birds) can be found in and around the water and sea ice. West Antarctica, including the western side of the Antarctic Peninsula, has a milder, more maritime climate influenced by the Pacific. Moss, lichens and algae can grow during a brief growing season. The subantarctic islands also have less harsh climates, and these are the breeding grounds for many birds, and lots of other penguin species.

In the water, the story changes again. Six species of seal live here, often seen hauled out on the rocks and ice, and six species of migratory whale live along with orcas, squid, countless krill and deep sea fish. But there are no land animals in Antarctica, and no native humans – the only people who live here do so in research stations, most of which are summer-only.

OPPOSITE:
Adélie penguins, Paulet Island, Antarctic Peninsula
Adélie penguins jump into freezing waters. Found right around Antarctica, these penguins can migrate around 13,000km (8,100 miles) each year as they move from their summer breeding colonies to winter hunting grounds – and then make the return journey.

RIGHT:

Adélie penguin chick crèche

These penguins need both ice and ice-free environments – they live on sea ice, but need the ice-free land to breed. As climate change reduces sea ice in Antarctica, Adélie penguin numbers have dropped by around 65 per cent in the last quarter of century.

OPPOSITE:

Adélie penguin colony, Weddell Sea

Adélie penguins breed in huge colonies, some featuring up to 250,000 pairs. To feed their growing chicks, these penguins must hunt and forage, mostly living on krill and fish.

**Adélie penguin on an
iceberg, Graham Passage**
Weighing up to 6kg (13lb),
Adélie penguins are generally
small but can be feisty. And
they can dive very well, to a
depth of 150m (492ft), for
around six minutes.

Blue-eyed shag
There are up to 14 species of
this bird. They feed on fish
and other seafood and can
dive to around 25m (82ft),
spending up to four minutes
under water. They often
feed in large numbers, called
a 'raft'.

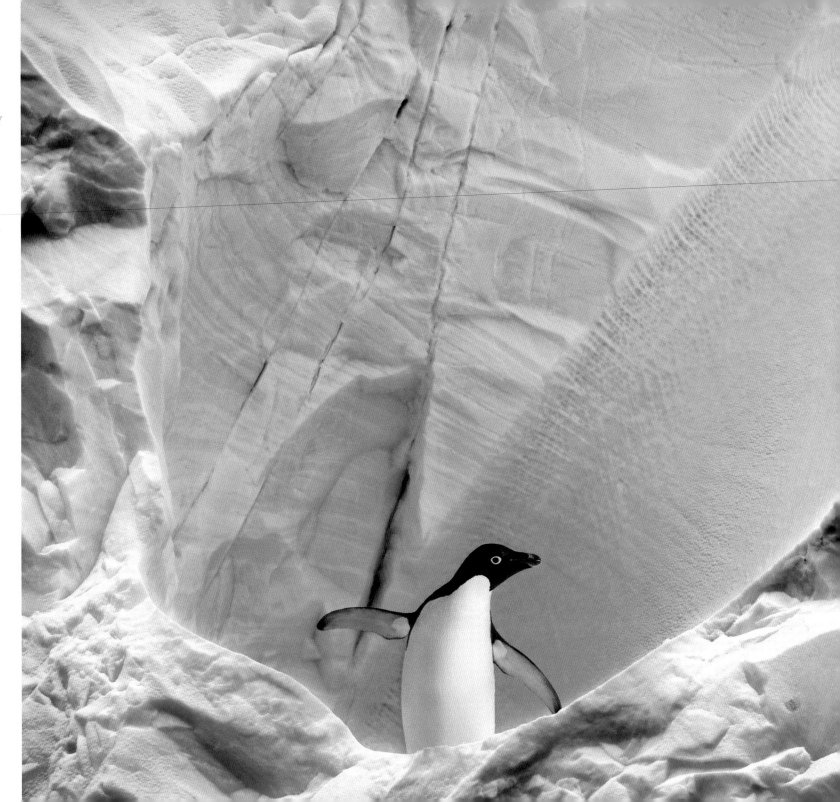

LEFT:

Black-browed albatross, South Georgia

The most common and widespread of the albatross family, this majestic seabird, also known as a mollyhawk, can live for 70 years. It can have a wingspan of up to 250cm (98in). There are about 600,000 breeding pairs, which eat fish and squid, as well as scavenge from trawlers.

RIGHT:

Nesting wandering albatross, South Georgia

The wandering albatross has the biggest wingspan of any bird, at around 310cm (126in), and is capable of covering an enormous 120,000km (75,000 miles) each year in the Southern Ocean. These seabirds mate for life and breed every two years on subantarctic islands. Classified as vulnerable, there are only 25,000 adult birds.

**Chinstrap penguins,
South Sandwich Islands**
Living on islands in the South
Pacific and the Antarctic, this
penguin is named after the
narrow black band under its
head. It grows up to 76cm
(30in) and weighs 5kg (11lb).

**Chinstrap penguins,
Antarctic Peninsula**
Chinstrap penguins' diet
consists of fish, krill, shrimp
and squid, and they will swim
long distances to find food,
around 80km (50 miles). But
as climate change impacts on
its environment, this penguin,
although not currently
threatened, may start to come
under pressure.

BOTH PHOTOGRAPHS:

Crabeater seals, Antarctic Peninsula
Despite their name, these seals eat krill rather than crabs.
They are highly sociable and will swim in groups of a hundred
or more – 1,000 have been seen hauled out on the ice. They
grow to more than 2m (6.6ft) in length and weigh up to 200kg
(440lb). Crabeater seal pups are preyed on by leopard seals –
up to 80 per cent of them will die. Despite this high death rate
there is a stable population of seven million of these seals.

Emperor penguin rookery, Snow Hill Island, Antarctic Peninsula

Emperor penguins are famous for their arduous treks, walking up to 120km (75 miles) over the ice to breeding colonies, which can contain several thousand birds. The female then lays a single egg, which is incubated for more than two months by the male, who eats nothing and must withstand the full force of the winter weather, losing about a quarter of his body weight, about 12kg (26lb), in the process. During this time, the female returns to the sea to feed and to bring back food.

LEFT:

Southern elephant seal, South Georgia, Antarctica
Getting its name from its huge size and large nose (the 'proboscis') of the adult male, bulls can grow up to 4,000kg (8,800lb) in weight and nearly 6m (20ft) in length. Females are only a quarter of the weight of bulls. Despite being hunted almost to extinction in the 19th century, there are now around 750,000 animals.

ABOVE:

Snowy sheathbill, South Georgia, Antarctica
The only land bird native to the Antarctic, snowy sheathbills, or 'mutts', are usually found on the ground. They scavenge and steal food and are known as the 'binmen of the Antarctic', eating anything that might make a meal, including penguin eggs and chicks, dead seals and animal faeces.

BOTH PHOTOGRAPHS:
Gentoo penguins
Around 90cm (35in) tall, gentoo penguins make nests from stones, which they arrange into a circular pile. The female lays two eggs, with the eggs hatching after five weeks (left). As adults, a few hundred birds will form a colony (opposite) on ice-free areas around beaches.

Humpback whales, Antarctic Peninsula
Humpback whales are migratory, often covering huge distances every year, up to 25,000km (16,000 miles). They are baleen (filter feeding) whales and arrive in both the Arctic and Antarctic in their respective summers to feed on small fish and huge amounts of krill.

BOTH PHOTOGRAPHS:

Orcas, Weddell Sea, Antarctic Peninsula

Also known as 'killer whales' (a misnomer, since orcas are a member of the dolphin family), orcas are highly social, hunting in 'pods' for fish, seals, turtles, seabirds and dolphins. One hunting technique is called 'spy-hopping' (right), in which the orcas create waves that will wash a resting seal into the water, where other orcas lie in wait. Adult males grow up to 8m (26ft) long and weigh over 6 tonnes (5.9 tons), while females are about two-thirds of that size.

King penguins on an iceberg
Looking much like its bigger relative the emperor penguin (apart from the solid orange patch on the cheek), the king penguin is the second-largest penguin, growing to around 100cm (39in) and weighing 12kg (26lb). It lives on milder, subantarctic islands and eats fish, squid and krill, diving to around 100m (330ft) – sometimes even more – for a meal. The total population is estimated to be over two million birds.

Krill

Krill are small crustaceans, up to 2cm (0.8in) long. They are near the bottom of the food chain and are a vital source of food for larger animals. The Antarctic krill has the largest total mass of any animal on the planet – there are 379 million tonnes (418 million tons) of krill in the ocean.

RIGHT:

Leopard seal

Also known as the sea leopard, most leopard seals stay in the pack ice throughout the year and are solitary creatures, hunting penguins, and the pups of other seal species. They can grow up to 3.5m (11.5ft) and weigh around 600kg (1,320lb).

Hauled out leopard seal and crabeater seal
Many seals, sea lions and walruses are often pictured lying on the ice. These animals literally haul themselves out of the water to breed, give birth and to rest. They may also haul out to avoid predators such as orcas, and to socialise.

RIGHT:

South polar skua

This predatory and scavenging seabird will feed on carcasses and kill penguin chicks, and has the hooked beak and sharp claws to be aggressive. With a wingspan of 121cm (48in), skuas are powerful and skilled flyers.

OPPOSITE:

Macaroni penguin colony, South Georgia, Antarctica

The macaroni is small, 70cm (28in) tall. But macaroni penguin breeding colonies are among the biggest of all the penguin varieties, sometimes numbering 100,000 birds. And with a population of approximately 18 million birds, the macaroni penguin is the most numerous of all the penguin species.

BOTH PHOTOGRAPHS:

Weddell seals
Often seen hauled out on sea ice (right) and found all the way around Antarctica, this large seal was named, like the Weddell Sea, after the early 19th-century British sealing captain, James Weddell. Growing up to 3.5m (11.5ft) long and weighing up to 600kg (1,320lb), Weddell seals can be found in small groups around holes in the ice with their heads sticking through (opposite), often to avoid harsh winter storms.

Picture Credits

Alamy: 8 (Jeffrey Miller), 11 (Colin Harris/era-images), 12 & 13 all (Biosphoto), 14/15 (Hemis), 16 (Danita Delimont), 17 (Hemis), 20 (Stocktrek Images), 38/39 (Xinhua), 46 (Stocktrek Images), 50/51 (Image Broker), 52 (Nature Picture Library), 54/55 (Stuart Holroyd), 56 (David Tipling Photo Library), 57 (John Digby), 75 (Boyd Norton), 76 & 77 all (All Canada Photos), 86/87 (Travelib Environment), 98 (Michael Grant), 110 (Martin Grace), 111 (James Cresswell), 114 (NASA Image Collection), 122/123 (Cavan Images), 127 (Blue Planet Archive), 129 (Blickwinkel), 130/131 (Steve Morgan), 138 (McPhoto/Bioquatic Photo), 145 (World Travel Collection), 146 (Blickwinkel), 148 (DOD Photo), 151 (Universal Images Group North America LLC/DeAgostini), 154 (Stocktrek Images), 156/157 (Nature Picture Library), 159 (Andy Myatt), 164 (Robert Harding), 166 (Colin Harris/era-images), 167 (Royal Geographic Society), 180 (Nature Picture Library), 181 (CTK), 189 top (Arctos Images), 189 bottom (Nature Picture Library), 194 (Jason Edwards), 196 (Steve Bloom Images), 206 (All Canada Photos), 210/211 (TheImage), 212 (Nature Picture Library), 213 (Nigel McCall), 216 (Dmytro Pylypenko), 221 (Samantha Crimmin)

Alamy/Minden Pictures: 40, 44/45, 47, 48/49, 67

Dreamstime: 6 (Vladimir Seliverstov), 19 (Darryn Schneider), 21 (Vlad32pa), 28 (Darryn Schneider), 30 (Mutabor5), 36/37 (Svalbord07), 53 (Darryn Schneider), 64/65 (Gentoomultimedia), 66 (Jonathan Green), 68/69 (Steve Allen), 70 (Photgrapherlondon), 71 (Steve Allen), 72 (Photographerlondon), 80 (Jocrebbin), 90 (Steve Allen), 92/93 (Letloose78), 94 (Jocrebbin), 95 (Tasfoto), 96/97 (Leltloose78), 104/105 (Hel080808), 106 & 107 (Steve Allen), 121 (William Perry), 124/125 (Steve Allen), 126 (Lorraine Kourafas), 134 (Steve Allen), 135 (Tas Foto), 136/137 (Lorraine Kourafas), 140 (Jonathan Green), 143 (Arne Beruldsen), 147 (Lisastrachan), 149 (Ahanson84), 162 (Derek Rogers), 170/171 (Guido Amrein), 173 (Derek Rogers), 177 (William Perry), 178/179 (Joe Sohm), 184 (Karen Foley), 186 & 188 (Martyn Unsworth), 191 (Cherylramalho), 195 (Barbarico), 201 (Mogens Trolle), 203 (Steve Gould), 207 (Mogens Trolle), 209 (Hel080808), 214 & 215 (Andrea Basile), 218/219 (Jonathan Green), 220 (Vivtoria Ivanets)

Dreamstime/Walter Steidenroth: 88, 89, 100, 112,113, 142, 197

Getty Images: 33 & 34 (Auscape), 73 & 74 (Wolfgang Kaehler), 91, 116 & 117 all (Mario Tama)

NASA: 18 (JPL-Caltech/UC Irvine), 58 (Jim Yungel), 59 (DMS/Nathan Kurtz), 114 both (Michael Studinger), 128 (Jesse Allen/Landsat data/U.S. Geological Survey), 144 (Earth Observatory/Natural Hazards), 152/153 (Brooke Medley)

Shutterstock: 7 (Rainer Lesniewski), 10 (Leland Mackay), 22–27 all (Sergey 402), 29 (Graeme Snow), 31 & 32 (polarman), 35 (Graeme Snow), 41 (GTW), 42 & 43 (sirtravelalot), 60/61 (Mesa Studios), 62/63 (Jeff Warneck), 78 (Robert McGilivray), 81 (Denis Burdin), 82/83 (Nick Pecker), 84 (TasfotoNL), 85 (Vadim Nefedoff), 99 (Gonzalo Solari Cooke), 101 (Bogorodskiy), 102 (Gonzalo Solari Cooke), 103 (Domicile Media), 108 & 109 (Marco Ramerini), 118 (Marc Andre Le Tourneux), 119 (FOTO 4440), 120 (Patrick Poendall), 132/133 (Ion Mes), 139 (Pole 2 Pole Images), 141 (Ion Mes), 150 (sergeydolya), 155 (Michael Lodge), 158 (Brian L Stetson), 160 (Mesa Studios), 161 (Wirestock Creators), 165 (Armin Rose), 168 (Marcos Amend), 169 (Philipp Salveter), 172 (HTN), 174/175 (Maksym Deliyergiyev), 176 (Yunus Toplal), 182 (Sergei Onyshko), 183 (Michail Vorobyev), 185 (James-stone76), 187 (Dale Lorna Jacobsen), 190 (John Carnemolla), 192 (Slowmotiongli), 198 (Danita Delimont), 199 & 200 (MZPHOTO.CZ), 202 (reisegraf.ch), 204/205 (Danita Delimont), 208 (Coral Brunner), 217, 222 (James-stone76), 223 (Vadim Nefedoff)